The Relevance of AT-Tawbah

Navigating Life's Trials as a Muslim

Zaytoona Nur

Copyright © *Zaytoona Nur*, 2025
All Rights Reserved

This book is subject to the condition that no part of this book is to be reproduced, transmitted in any form or means; electronic or mechanical, stored in a retrieval system, photocopied, recorded, scanned, or otherwise. Any of these actions require the proper written permission of the author.

Table of Contents

Chapter 1: Understanding At-Tawbah 1

Chapter 2: The Concept of Repentance in Islam 5

Chapter 3: At-Tawbah and Personal Growth 9

Chapter 4: At-Tawbah in the Face of Trials 13

Chapter 5: Community and Support in Repentance 17

Chapter 6: Practical Applications of At-Tawbah 21

Chapter 7: At-Tawbah and Forgiveness 24

Chapter 8: The Future of At-Tawbah in Muslim Life 28

Chapter 9: Conclusion: Embracing At-Tawbah 32

Chapter 1:

Understanding At-Tawbah

Definition and Significance

At Tawbah, often referred to as "The Repentance," holds a pivotal place in Islamic teachings, signifying both a spiritual and moral compass for Muslims. The term itself encapsulates the process of returning to God after committing sins or mistakes, underpinning the essence of seeking forgiveness and rectication in one's life. This concept is not merely about the act of repentance; it embodies a broader understanding of accountability, self-awareness, and the continuous journey toward spiritual growth. At-Tawbah serves as a reminder of the inherent imperfections of humanity and the ever- available opportunity for redemption.

The significance of At-Tawbah extends beyond individual acts of contrition. It emphasises the relational aspect of human existence, focusing on the connection between the individual and the divine. In a world where moral complexities abound, the teachings of At-Tawbah guide Muslims in navigating their trials and tribulations. The underlying principle of turning back to God fosters resilience, encouraging believers to confront their shortcomings and strive for betterment. This process is vital not only for personal development but also for fostering a sense of community and collective responsibility among Muslims.

In contemporary society, where distractions and moral dilemmas are prevalent, the relevance of At-Tawbah becomes even more pronounced. The pressures of modern life can lead to feelings of isolation and despair, making the act of seeking forgiveness and returning to one's faith a powerful antidote. By understanding At-Tawbah, individuals can find solace in their struggles and realise that they are not alone in their journey. This realisation has the potential to transform personal crises into opportunities for spiritual enlightenment, ultimately strengthening one's faith in challenging times.

Moreover, At-Tawbah underscores the importance of intention in the repentance process. It is not merely the act of saying sorry; it involves a sincere commitment to change and a heartfelt desire to improve oneself. This aspect of At-Tawbah encourages self-reflection and mindfulness, prompting individuals to assess their actions and their impact on themselves and others. In doing so, it fosters a culture of accountability and integrity, essential values in today's interconnected world, where actions have far-reaching consequences.

Finally, the teachings of At-Tawbah can serve as a guiding framework for Muslims in their everyday lives, providing tools to navigate both personal and communal challenges. By incorporating its principles into daily routines, believers can cultivate a mindset of continuous improvement and compassion. The significance of At-Tawbah lies not only in its spiritual implications but also in its practical applications, fostering a holistic approach to life that harmonises faith with action. This integration helps individuals not only to seek forgiveness but also to extend grace to others, nurturing a more empathetic and understanding society.

Historical Context

The chapter on historical context provides a framework for understanding Surah At-Tawbah within the broader narrative of Islamic history. Revealed in the year 9 AH (after Hijrah), this Surah addresses pivotal events following the establishment of the Muslim community in Medina. It was a period marked by significant challenges, including wars, the consolidation of political power, and the need for clear guidelines regarding community conduct. The historical backdrop of At-Tawbah highlights the transition from a nascent community to a more organised society that faced external threats and internal dissent.

At-Tawbah stands out as the only chapter in the Quran that does not begin with "Bismillah" (In the name of Allah). This absence is often interpreted as a reflection of the serious tone and the gravity of the circumstances addressed within its verses. The Surah deals with the aftermath of the Battle of Tabuk, where the Muslim community faced a crucial test of faith and commitment. The historical events surrounding this battle illustrate the challenges of leadership and the necessity of unity among believers in times of strife.

The Surah also addresses the issue of hypocrisy within the community. During the time of the Prophet Muhammad (SAW), some individuals claimed to be Muslims while secretly undermining the community's efforts. At-Tawbah explicitly calls out these hypocrites and emphasises the importance of sincerity and loyalty to the Muslim Ummah. This context is crucial for contemporary readers as it underscores the ongoing relevance of integrity and faithfulness within the modern Muslim experience.

Furthermore, At-Tawbah introduces significant themes such as repentance, mercy, and social justice. The historical context reveals how these themes were not merely abstract concepts but were grounded in the realities of the time. The Surah calls upon believers to seek forgiveness and to engage in acts of charity, reinforcing the notion that personal and communal responsibility are intertwined. This understanding is vital for Muslims today, as they navigate their spiritual journeys and societal obligations.

Finally, the relevance of At-Tawbah extends beyond its historical context; it serves as a timeless reminder of the trials faced by the early Muslim community. The teachings encapsulated within this Surah offer guidance on how to confront adversity, maintain faith, and foster a sense of community. In a world marked by division and uncertainty, the principles found in At-Tawbah encourage Muslims to reflect on their own lives, reinforcing the idea that the lessons of the past continue to inform and inspire contemporary Muslim identity and resilience.

Key Themes in At-Tawbah

At-Tawbah, the ninth chapter of the Quran, presents several key themes that resonate deeply with the lives of Muslims today. One of the central themes is the concept of repentance and forgiveness, which plays a crucial role in the spiritual journey of individuals. The chapter emphasises that no matter how far one has strayed, sincere repentance can lead to divine forgiveness. This theme is particularly relevant in contemporary society, where individuals often struggle with guilt and the burden of their past actions. At-Tawbah encourages believers to seek forgiveness not just from Allah, but also from those they may have wronged, fostering a sense of accountability and community.

Another significant theme in At-Tawbah is the importance of sincerity in faith and actions. The chapter calls for Muslims to engage in their beliefs wholeheartedly, devoid of hypocrisy. In a world filled with distractions and competing ideologies, the call to authenticity remains pertinent. At-Tawbah challenges individuals to reflect on their intentions and ensure that their actions align with their faith. This theme encourages believers to cultivate a genuine relationship with their Creator, which is essential for personal growth and spiritual fulfilment.

The chapter also addresses the concept of community and collective responsibility. At-Tawbah highlights the importance of standing together as a community, particularly during times of trial and adversity. This theme is significant in today's context, where societal challenges often require a united response. The text reminds Muslims of the need to support one another, whether through acts of charity, standing against injustice, or providing moral support. By emphasising communal ties, At-Tawbah reinforces the idea that individual actions have collective implications, thus advocating for a more engaged and responsible community.

Furthermore, At-Tawbah discusses the balance between mercy and justice, illustrating how both qualities are essential in Islam. The chapter reflects on the importance of upholding justice while also being compassionate towards those who have erred. This theme is crucial in contemporary discussions surrounding social justice and equity.

Muslims are encouraged to advocate for fairness in society while embodying mercy in their personal interactions. The challenge lies in navigating these dual aspects, and At-Tawbah provides guidance on how to maintain this balance in daily life.

Lastly, the theme of perseverance in faith during trials is prominent in At-Tawbah. The chapter encourages believers to remain steadfast in their beliefs, even when faced with difficulties. It underscores the idea that trials can serve as tests of one's faith and can ultimately lead to spiritual elevation. In an age where many face various challenges, from personal struggles to global issues, this theme serves as a reminder of the resilience required to navigate life's complexities. At-Tawbah inspires Muslims to draw strength from their faith, assuring them that perseverance is rewarded, both in this life and the hereafter.

Chapter 2:

The Concept of Repentance in Islam

The Nature of Sin

Sin, in various religious and philosophical contexts, is often understood as an act that deviates from a moral or divine standard. Within Islamic teachings, sin is not merely a social or legal infraction but a profound violation of the relationship between the individual and Allah. The concept of sin encompasses actions, intentions, and even thoughts that distance a person from divine guidance. Understanding sin in this holistic manner emphasises that it is not solely about the act itself but also about the state of the heart and mind, which are integral to the Islamic faith.

Islam categorises sins into major and minor types, with major sins (kaba'ir) being those that have severe repercussions both in this life and the hereafter. Examples of major sins include polytheism, murder, and theft. Minor sins (saghā'ir), while still considered wrong, are viewed as less severe and can be forgiven through repentance, good deeds, and the mercy of Allah. This categorisation serves to illustrate that while all sin is serious, the gravity of certain actions necessitates a more urgent and sincere repentance. Recognising this distinction can guide individuals in their journey towards spiritual growth and moral rectitude.

The nature of sin also invites contemplation on the human condition. Islamic teachings acknowledge that humans are fallible and prone to error; thus, the experience of sin is universal. The Qur'an and Hadith provide numerous examples of prophets and righteous figures who committed errors, underscoring the reality that sin is part of the human experience. This understanding fosters a compassionate view of oneself and others, encouraging believers to approach sin with humility rather than despair. It is through acknowledging our imperfections that we can fully appreciate the concept of repentance (Tawbah) and the mercy of Allah.

Repentance in Islam is not just about seeking forgiveness; it is a transformative process that involves regret, cessation of the sinful act, and a rm intention not to return to that sin. This process is vital for spiritual growth and the restoration of one's relationship with Allah. The nature of sin, then, becomes a catalyst for personal reform. By confronting our sins and understanding their impact on our lives and spirituality, we can cultivate a deeper connection with our faith and a more profound sense of accountability.

In contemporary life, the relevance of understanding sin goes beyond religious doctrine; it informs ethical decision-making and personal conduct in a rapidly changing world. As Muslims navigate the complexities of modern society, the principles surrounding sin and repentance can serve as a moral compass. They encourage individuals to strive for integrity and righteousness in their actions, fostering a community that values accountability and compassion. Ultimately, recognising the nature of sin allows Muslims to embrace the path of Tawbah as a continuous journey towards self-improvement and a closer relationship with Allah.

The Process of Repentance

Repentance, or At-Tawbah, is a profound concept deeply rooted in Islamic teachings. It serves as a mechanism for individuals to reconnect with their faith and seek forgiveness for their transgressions. Understanding the process of repentance involves recognising its stages, which include acknowledgement of one's sins, feeling genuine remorse, making a firm intention to change, and seeking forgiveness from Allah. Each stage plays a crucial role in the journey toward spiritual renewal and personal growth, offering a pathway to overcome the challenges that life presents.

The first step in the process of repentance is the acknowledgement of one's sins. This requires a level of self-awareness and honesty that can be difficult for many individuals. It involves reflecting on one's actions and recognising the areas where one has deviated from the principles of Islam. This acknowledgement is not merely about identifying wrongdoings; it is about understanding the impact these actions have on oneself and on relationships with others. By admitting to shortcomings, individuals take a crucial step toward healing and transformation.

Following acknowledgement, the next stage is experiencing genuine remorse for one's actions. This remorse is not just a fleeting feeling of guilt; it is a profound emotional response that indicates a true understanding of the severity of one's sins. In Islam, remorse is vital as it signifies a heart that is aware and sensitive to the consequences of its actions. This stage fosters a desire to seek forgiveness, not only from Allah but also from those who may have been affected by one's actions. Such empathy and compassion are essential components of a sincere repentance process.

The third critical step is making a firm intention to change. This involves a commitment to avoiding the same sins in the future and actively working towards self-improvement. It is here that individuals must engage in practical actions to reinforce their intention, such as increasing their acts of worship, seeking knowledge, and surrounding themselves with positive influences. This commitment is not simply about abstaining from sins but is also about cultivating a character aligned with Islamic values. The intention to improve oneself is a crucial element that transforms the process of repentance from a mere ritual into a genuine act of faith.

Finally, seeking forgiveness from Allah is the culmination of the repentance process. This step can be performed through prayer, supplication, and heartfelt communication with the Divine. Islamic teachings emphasise the importance of sincerity in this act, as Allah's mercy is vast and encompasses all who earnestly seek it. It is also essential to maintain a spirit of humility during this process, recognising that forgiveness is a gift from Allah and that one must remain steadfast in their efforts to uphold their intention to change. By embracing repentance, individuals not only find solace but also gain strength to navigate life's trials with renewed faith and resilience.

The Role of Intention

The concept of intention, or niyyah, serves as a foundational principle in Islam, influencing the actions and decisions of individuals. Intention is not merely about the act itself but encapsulates the purpose behind each action. In the context of At-Tawbah, the act of repentance, intention plays a critical role in determining the sincerity and authenticity of one's return to Allah. It is through a genuine intention that a believer can truly embrace the transformative power of repentance, aligning their actions with their spiritual goals and aspirations.

In Islamic teachings, actions are judged not only by their outcomes but also by the intentions that underpin them. The famous hadith, "Actions are judged by intentions," emphasises that the intention behind an act can elevate its spiritual value. When applying this understanding to At-Tawbah, it becomes evident that the sincerity of one's repentance is significantly influenced by the intention to seek forgiveness and reform. This intention propels individuals to reflect on their past actions, recognises their shortcomings, and commit to positive change, fostering a cycle of growth and spiritual renewal.

The role of intention extends beyond the personal realm; it also influences one's interactions with others and the broader community. When individuals approach their relationships and responsibilities with sincere intentions, they foster an environment of trust, compassion, and understanding. In the context of At-Tawbah, this means not only seeking forgiveness for one's own misdeeds but also striving to mend broken relationships and contribute positively to the community. The intention to support and uplift others can transform individual repentance into a collective journey towards spiritual and social harmony.

Moreover, intention serves as a guiding principle in navigating the trials and tribulations of life. In contemporary society, where distractions and temptations abound, maintaining a clear and focused intention can help individuals stay grounded in their faith. By regularly revisiting and reaffirming their intentions, Muslims can better resist negative influences and remain committed to their spiritual goals. This conscious effort to align one's intentions with Islamic values can lead to a more fulfilling and purpose-driven life, even amid challenges and adversities.

Ultimately, the power of intention in the context of At-Tawbah is profound. It acts as a catalyst for genuine self-reflection, personal growth, and communal responsibility. As individuals strive to refine their intentions, they can cultivate a deeper connection with Allah and a more meaningful existence. Understanding that every act, whether small or significant, carries weight based on one's intention encourages Muslims to approach life with mindfulness and sincerity, reinforcing the relevance of At-Tawbah in contemporary Muslim life.

Chapter 3:

At-Tawbah and Personal Growth

Lessons in Humility

Humility is a fundamental virtue that is emphasised in Islamic teachings, particularly in the context of repentance and self-reflection as highlighted in At-Tawbah. This chapter delves into the essential lessons in humility that can be drawn from the themes of this significant surah. At-Tawbah encourages believers to recognise their shortcomings and to approach life with a mindset of humility. This self-awareness fosters a deeper connection with Allah and enhances one's character in the face of trials.

One of the primary lessons in humility is the recognition of human fallibility. The surah acknowledges that all individuals are prone to errors and misjudgments. This understanding invites believers to embrace their imperfections and to seek forgiveness sincerely. It highlights the importance of acknowledging one's limitations and the need to turn to Allah for guidance and support. In contemporary life, where perfectionism is often glorified, embracing our flaws can lead to personal growth and the development of empathy towards others who also struggle.

Another significant aspect of humility as illustrated in At-Tawbah is the importance of community and collective responsibility. The surah calls on the Muslim community to support one another in times of difficulty and to hold each other accountable. This collective approach fosters a sense of belonging and encourages individuals to set aside their egos for the bene t of the group. By prioritising the welfare of others, individuals learn to humble themselves, recognising that their actions impact the broader community. In modern contexts, this lesson serves as a reminder of the value of teamwork and cooperation in overcoming challenges.

Furthermore, humility cultivates gratitude, a recurring theme within the surah. A humble heart is one that acknowledges the countless blessings bestowed by Allah, leading to a life filled with appreciation. This sense of gratitude is vital in navigating life's trials, as it shifts focus from what one lacks to what one has. It encourages individuals to be thankful for both the highs and lows of life, understanding that each experience is part of a divine plan. In today's fast-paced world, where discontent can easily arise, this lesson is particularly relevant, promoting mental and spiritual well-being.

Lastly, humility nurtures resilience in the face of adversity. At-Tawbah teaches that trials are a means of purification and growth, and approaching these challenges with humility allows individuals to learn valuable lessons. Rather than succumbing to despair, a humble person seeks to understand the wisdom behind their struggles, using them as opportunities for self-improvement. This perspective is crucial in contemporary life, where individuals often face significant stress and uncertainty. By adopting a humble attitude, one can navigate difficulties with grace, ultimately emerging stronger and more grounded in faith.

Building Resilience

Building resilience is a vital aspect of navigating life's trials, particularly within the framework of At-Tawbah. This concept, derived from the Quran, emphasises the importance of repentance and returning to one's faith amidst adversity. Resilience is not merely about enduring hardship; it involves the ability to bounce back, learn, and grow from difficulties. For Muslims, integrating the principles of At-Tawbah into everyday life can provide a spiritual foundation that strengthens their resolve when faced with challenges.

One fundamental aspect of building resilience through At-Tawbah is the focus on self-reflection and accountability. The act of repentance encourages individuals to examine their actions and intentions. This self-assessment fosters a deeper understanding of personal strengths and weaknesses, allowing individuals to recognise areas for improvement. By acknowledging past mistakes and actively seeking forgiveness, a Muslim can cultivate a mindset that sees challenges as opportunities for growth rather than insurmountable obstacles.

Another essential component is the role of community and support in resilience. At-Tawbah emphasises the importance of returning to God and seeking His guidance, but it also highlights the value of communal bonds. Engaging with fellow believers provides a network of support during difficult times. Sharing experiences and seeking advice from others can reinforce one's faith and resilience. The collective strength of a community can uplift individuals, reminding them that they are not alone in their struggles and that support is always available.

Spiritual practices such as prayer, reflection, and seeking knowledge are integral to developing resilience. These practices serve as tools for grounding oneself in faith and providing clarity amid chaos. Regular engagement with the teachings of the Quran can inspire hope and reassure individuals that trials are a part of life's journey. Additionally, understanding the stories of the Prophets and their unwavering faith during adversity can serve as powerful examples to draw strength from, illustrating that perseverance in faith leads to eventual success.

Finally, building resilience through At-Tawbah involves a commitment to continuous improvement and growth. Life's trials often serve as catalysts for personal development. Embracing the lessons learned through hardship can lead to a more profound faith and a better understanding of one's purpose. By recognising that challenges are opportunities for spiritual elevation, Muslims can approach difficulties with a renewed sense of purpose and determination. This perspective not only enhances individual resilience but also contributes to a more robust community that can face trials together with faith and fortitude.

The Journey of Self-Improvement

The journey of self-improvement is a profound and ongoing process that shapes an individual's character, values, and overall life experience. For Muslims, this journey is deeply intertwined with the principles of At-Tawbah, or repentance. At-Tawbah offers a framework for recognising shortcomings and striving for betterment, emphasising the importance of self-reflection, accountability, and the pursuit of righteousness. This journey is not merely about personal growth; it is a spiritual endeavour that seeks to align one's actions with divine guidance and moral integrity.

Central to the concept of self-improvement is the acknowledgement of one's flaws and the willingness to change. At-Tawbah encourages individuals to examine their behaviour, thoughts, and intentions critically. This introspection is essential for identifying negative patterns and habits that may hinder personal and spiritual growth. By embracing the practice of repentance, Muslims can confront their shortcomings with honesty and humility, facilitating a transformative process that fosters resilience and a deeper connection to their faith.

The relevance of At-Tawbah in contemporary Muslim life extends beyond individual improvement; it also encompasses communal responsibility. As individuals embark on their journeys of self-improvement, they contribute to the betterment of their families, communities, and society at large. The collective impact of personal growth can lead to a more compassionate and understanding community, where individuals support one another in their efforts to adhere to Islamic principles. This sense of unity is vital in navigating the challenges of modern life, where distractions and moral dilemmas are ubiquitous.

Moreover, the journey of self-improvement is not linear; it is characterised by struggles, setbacks, and moments of clarity. At-Tawbah serves as a reminder that the path to righteousness is fraught with challenges, yet each attempt at repentance is a step toward healing and renewal. This understanding encourages individuals to be patient with themselves and to recognise that setbacks are a natural part of the growth process. The act of returning to Allah through repentance is a source of strength, reinforcing the belief that transformation is possible regardless of past mistakes.

In conclusion, the journey of self-improvement is an essential aspect of contemporary Muslim life, intricately linked to the principles of At-Tawbah. By embracing the process of self-reflection, accountability, and communal responsibility, individuals can cultivate a sense of purpose and fulfilment. This journey not only enhances personal character but also strengthens the bonds within the community, creating an environment where mutual support and understanding thrive. Ultimately, At-Tawbah guides Muslims towards a more meaningful and spiritually enriched life, emphasising the importance of striving for continuous growth and improvement.

Chapter 4:

At-Tawbah in the Face of Trials

Understanding Life's Challenges

Life is inherently filled with challenges that test our resilience, character, and faith. For many, these trials can feel overwhelming and isolating. Understanding life's challenges, particularly from a spiritual perspective, is essential for navigating through them effectively. The concept of At-Tawbah, or repentance, provides a framework for Muslims to confront their difficulties with a sense of purpose and clarity. It allows individuals to recognise their shortcomings and seek forgiveness, which is a vital step in overcoming personal and communal trials.

At-Tawbah encourages reflection on one's actions and intentions. In facing life's challenges, one can often lose sight of their core values and beliefs. By engaging in self-assessment and repentance, individuals can reconnect with their faith and gain a deeper understanding of their circumstances. This process not only fosters personal growth but also strengthens the connection with the community. When individuals acknowledge their struggles and seek to improve themselves, they set a precedent for others to do the same, creating a supportive atmosphere for collective healing.

Moreover, challenges often serve as a catalyst for change. They compel individuals to reassess their priorities and realign their goals with their values. The teachings of At-Tawbah emphasise the importance of perseverance in the face of adversity. When Muslims encounter trials, they are reminded that these experiences are opportunities for spiritual elevation. Embracing challenges as part of a divine plan can transform one's perspective, allowing for a more profound appreciation of life's lessons and the wisdom that emerges from hardship.

The communal aspect of challenges is also significant. Life's trials are not experienced in isolation; they affect families, friends, and communities. At-Tawbah highlights the importance of supporting one another during difficult times. By fostering a spirit of compassion and understanding, Muslims can create an environment where individuals feel safe to share their struggles. This communal support not only alleviates the burden of hardship but also reinforces the bonds of faith and fellowship within the community, reminding everyone that they are not alone in their trials.

Finally, understanding and embracing life's challenges through the lens of At-Tawbah can lead to a more profound sense of fulfilment and peace. The journey of repentance is not merely about seeking forgiveness; it is about transformation and resilience. As individuals navigate their trials, they can emerge stronger and more aligned with their purpose. In doing so, they reflect the essence of their faith, demonstrating the relevance of At-Tawbah in contemporary Muslim life. By viewing challenges as opportunities for growth, Muslims can cultivate a resilient spirit that not only endures hardship but thrives through it.

Spiritual Strength During Adversity

Spiritual strength during adversity is a critical aspect of navigating life's trials, particularly from an Islamic perspective. In the context of At-Tawbah, which emphasises repentance and returning to Allah, believers are reminded that adversity often serves as a test of faith and resilience. The Quranic teachings encourage individuals to view hardships as opportunities for spiritual growth rather than purely as setbacks. This understanding fosters a mindset that seeks to draw closer to Allah during difficult times, reinforcing the idea that every trial can lead to a deeper connection with the divine.

In times of adversity, Muslims are urged to engage in sincere repentance and self-reflection, central themes in At-Tawbah. This process not only involves acknowledging one's shortcomings but also committing to personal growth and improvement. The act of turning back to Allah provides a source of comfort and strength. Believers are reminded that they are not alone in their struggles and that seeking forgiveness can lead to a sense of peace and clarity. This spiritual practice helps to cultivate resilience, enabling individuals to face challenges with a renewed sense of purpose.

Moreover, the concept of patience, or Sabr, is integral to developing spiritual strength during trials. The Quran repeatedly emphasises the importance of patience in the face of adversity, illustrating that it is through enduring hardships with grace that one can attain spiritual elevation. This patience is not merely passive endurance; it is an active engagement with one's circumstances, seeking understanding and maintaining faith. The teachings of the Prophet Muhammad also reinforce this idea, highlighting that those who remain steadfast are rewarded both in this life and the Hereafter.

Community support plays a vital role in enhancing spiritual strength during difficult times. Engaging with fellow Muslims, sharing experiences, and providing mutual support can significantly bolster an individual's resolve. The principles found in At-Tawbah encourage believers to maintain strong ties within their communities, reminding them that collective worship, prayer, and acts of charity can help alleviate personal burdens. When individuals come together to support one another, they create an environment that nurtures spiritual growth and resilience, making the challenges faced more bearable.

Ultimately, spiritual strength during adversity is a transformative experience that can lead to a more profound understanding of oneself and a closer relationship with Allah. The relevance of At-Tawbah in contemporary Muslim life highlights the importance of repentance, patience, and community in navigating trials. By embracing these concepts, individuals can cultivate resilience and emerge from their challenges not only unscathed but enriched in faith and character. This journey of spiritual growth during adversity is a testament to the enduring power of faith in the face of life's difficulties.

Seeking Forgiveness and Healing

Forgiveness and healing are central themes in the journey of repentance, often referred to as At-Tawbah in Islamic teachings. Seeking forgiveness involves acknowledging one's mistakes and turning towards Allah with sincerity and humility. This act is not merely a ritualistic recitation of words but a profound commitment to change and personal growth. In contemporary Muslim life, where challenges and trials abound, the process of seeking forgiveness can serve as a powerful catalyst for healing both oneself and one's relationships with others.

Forgiveness in Islam is deeply rooted in the understanding that all humans are fallible. The Quran emphasises that Allah is the Most Forgiving, extending mercy to those who earnestly seek it. This divine attribute serves as a reminder for Muslims to emulate this quality in their interactions with others. Forgiving others becomes a means of liberating oneself from the burdens of resentment and anger, fostering a sense of peace and emotional well-being. By forgiving others, individuals can create a healthier environment, conducive to healing and personal growth.

The journey towards healing often begins with self-reflection. Individuals must confront their own mistakes and understand the impact of their actions on themselves and others. This process requires honesty and courage, as it involves recognising areas where one has strayed from the path of righteousness. Engaging in sincere repentance not only strengthens one's relationship with Allah but also cultivates a sense of accountability and responsibility. This accountability is crucial in contemporary life, where distractions and societal pressures can lead individuals away from their core values.

In seeking forgiveness, it is important to establish a plan for personal development.

This involves setting realistic goals to avoid repeating past mistakes and fostering positive habits. Engaging in acts of worship, such as prayer and community service, can reinforce one's commitment to change. Moreover, seeking guidance from knowledgeable individuals or scholars can provide valuable insights and support during this transformative process. The act of seeking forgiveness and striving for improvement is an ongoing endeavour that enriches one's spiritual life and enhances overall well-being.

Ultimately, the process of seeking forgiveness and healing is intertwined with the broader concept of At-Tawbah. It highlights the significance of personal responsibility, the power of mercy, and the importance of community support in a Muslim's life. By embracing forgiveness, both from Allah and towards others, individuals can navigate life's trials with resilience and grace. This journey not only leads to personal fulfilment but also strengthens the bonds within the community, promoting a culture of understanding, compassion, and mutual support.

Chapter 5:

Community and Support in Repentance

The Role of Family and Friends

The role of family and friends is pivotal in navigating life's trials, especially within the context of At-Tawbah. The concept of At-Tawbah, or repentance, emphasises the importance of community support in overcoming personal challenges and spiritual shortcomings. Family and friends serve as the first line of support and guidance, offering a sense of belonging and encouragement during difficult times. Their influence often shapes an individual's understanding of faith and the practice of At-Tawbah, reinforcing the idea that seeking forgiveness is not a solitary endeavour but a collective journey.

In many Muslim cultures, family bonds are deeply rooted in shared beliefs and values. This connection is crucial when individuals face trials that test their faith. Family members can provide a safe space for open discussions about struggles, facilitating an environment where one feels comfortable seeking guidance and understanding. The shared commitment to practising At-Tawbah can lead to collective reflections on personal failures and the importance of seeking forgiveness from Allah. This communal approach not only strengthens familial ties but also enhances spiritual growth and resilience.

Friends also play a significant role in supporting each other through life's challenges, particularly in times of hardship. The bonds of friendship often provide a unique perspective, as friends may offer insights that family members might overlook. Engaging in discussions about At-Tawbah with friends can inspire individuals to confront their shortcomings and strive for improvement. These interactions can be a source of motivation, as friends can hold each other accountable, encouraging a continuous commitment to personal growth and repentance.

Furthermore, the role of family and friends extends beyond emotional support; they can also act as role models in practising At-Tawbah. Observing how loved ones navigate their own trials and seek forgiveness can instil a sense of hope and determination in individuals facing similar struggles. This modelling behaviour reinforces the principles of At-Tawbah, illustrating the transformative power of repentance and the importance of maintaining strong relationships with those who share similar values. The collective experience of overcoming challenges together fosters a spirit of unity and shared purpose.

Ultimately, the significance of family and friends in the context of At-Tawbah cannot be overstated. Their support structures create a nurturing environment that enhances personal and communal faith. By actively engaging in discussions about repentance and shared experiences, individuals can deepen their understanding of At-Tawbah and its relevance in contemporary life. This collective approach not only uplifts individuals facing trials but also fortifies the broader community, fostering a culture of understanding, compassion, and spiritual growth.

Building a Supportive Community

Building a supportive community is essential for navigating life's trials, especially for Muslims seeking to adhere to the principles outlined in At-Tawbah. A supportive community provides a network of individuals who uplift each other, share wisdom, and offer assistance during challenging times. In contemporary society, where isolation and disconnection can often prevail, fostering such communities becomes increasingly important. This subchapter explores the significance of community and practical steps to cultivate a nurturing environment that aligns with the teachings of At-Tawbah.

At-Tawbah emphasises the importance of sincere relationships based on mutual support and trust. The Quran encourages believers to come together in faith and righteousness, reinforcing the idea that community is not just a social construct but a spiritual obligation. In times of personal or collective struggles, having a network of individuals who embody these values can provide comfort and guidance. This communal bond fosters resilience, allowing individuals to navigate challenges with a sense of belonging and shared purpose.

One of the fundamental aspects of building a supportive community is open communication. Encouraging honest discussions about struggles, doubts, and experiences can help break down barriers and foster empathy among community members. When individuals feel safe to share their challenges, it creates an atmosphere of understanding and solidarity. This openness not only strengthens relationships but also cultivates a culture of support where members actively seek to help one another in overcoming difficulties.

Moreover, community activities play a crucial role in strengthening ties among members. Organising events such as study circles, social gatherings, and volunteer opportunities can enhance relationships and promote collective growth. These initiatives encourage collaboration and provide opportunities for individuals to contribute their skills and knowledge. When community members engage in meaningful activities together, they develop deeper connections that can prove invaluable during times of trial.

In conclusion, building a supportive community rooted in the principles of At-Tawbah is vital for Muslims navigating life's challenges. By fostering open communication, encouraging participation in community activities, and nurturing relationships based on trust and mutual support, individuals can create a resilient network that thrives on collective strength. Such a community not only aids in overcoming personal trials but also reinforces the shared values of faith and compassion, essential for a fulfilling and balanced life.

Collective Repentance and Growth

Collective repentance, or Tawbah, within a community context plays a crucial role in fostering spiritual growth and unity among its members. When individuals come together to acknowledge their shortcomings and seek forgiveness, they create a supportive environment that encourages self-improvement and accountability. This collective act of turning back to Allah not only strengthens personal faith but also reinforces the bonds between community members. By recognising their shared struggles and committing to a path of righteousness together, communities can cultivate a sense of belonging and collective responsibility.

The importance of collective repentance can be seen in its ability to create a culture of humility and openness within a community. When individuals witness others expressing remorse for their actions, it can inspire them to reflect on their own behaviours and shortcomings. This mutual exchange of vulnerability fosters an atmosphere where members feel safe to discuss their challenges without fear of judgment. Through this process, communities can confront social issues, such as injustice or disunity, and work collectively toward solutions that align with Islamic values. This collective awareness empowers individuals to take ownership of their actions and encourages them to strive for personal and communal betterment.

Furthermore, collective repentance serves as a catalyst for growth by encouraging community engagement and collaboration. When groups gather for repentance, they often engage in discussions on how to improve their collective well-being, which can lead to initiatives aimed at serving the community. These initiatives can range from charity work to educational programs, all stemming from a desire to rectify past shortcomings and build a brighter future. Engaging in such activities not only aids in healing the community but also reinforces the values of compassion, empathy, and solidarity that are central to Islamic teachings.

The process of collective repentance also provides an opportunity for education and awareness. Communities can use this time to discuss the significance of repentance in Islam, exploring its roots in the Quran and Hadith. Such discussions can deepen the understanding of Tawbah and its implications for contemporary life. By framing repentance as an ongoing journey rather than a one-time event, communities can encourage continuous self-reflection and growth among their members. This educational aspect ensures that the principles of Tawbah are woven into the fabric of community life, making them relevant in daily interactions and decisions.

In conclusion, collective repentance is essential for fostering growth within a community and enhancing the relevance of Tawbah in contemporary Muslim life. It encourages individuals to confront their shortcomings, promotes a culture of empathy and support, and motivates collective action for positive change. As communities come together to seek forgiveness and work towards improvement, they embody the essence of Islamic teachings and create a nurturing environment for all members to thrive spiritually and socially. Embracing collective repentance not only benefits the individuals involved but also enriches the entire community, paving the way for a more united and resilient society.

Chapter 6:

Practical Applications of At-Tawbah

Daily Practices for Repentance

Daily practices for repentance serve as essential tools for Muslims seeking to maintain a strong spiritual connection and navigate life's challenges. At-Tawbah, or repentance, is not merely a one-time act but a continuous journey that requires dedication and sincerity. Engaging in daily practices can help individuals cultivate a mindset of humility and awareness, allowing them to recognise their shortcomings and strive for improvement. These practices create a structured way to reflect on one's actions and seek forgiveness from Allah, fostering spiritual growth and resilience.

One of the foundational daily practices for repentance is the establishment of regular prayer, or Salah. The five daily prayers serve as a reminder of one's relationship with Allah and provide opportunities to seek forgiveness. During these moments of worship, individuals can reflect on their day, acknowledge their mistakes, and sincerely ask for Allah's mercy. Incorporating additional voluntary prayers, such as the Tahajjud prayer during the night, can further enhance this practice, allowing for deeper reflection and personal connection with the Divine.

Another effective practice is the recitation of Quranic verses and supplications specifically related to repentance. Verses that emphasise Allah's mercy and forgiveness can instil hope and motivate individuals to turn back to Him. Additionally, the use of du'as, or personal supplications, allows for a heartfelt expression of remorse and a request for guidance. By integrating these elements into their daily routine, individuals can actively engage in the process of At-Tawbah, reinforcing their commitment to spiritual growth and self-improvement.

Self-reflection is a crucial component of daily repentance practices. Taking time each day to assess one's actions, intentions, and thoughts encourages individuals to confront their shortcomings honestly. This practice can involve journaling, meditating, or simply spending quiet time in contemplation. By identifying specific areas for improvement, individuals can set realistic goals for themselves and actively work towards becoming better versions of themselves. This self-awareness not only aids in personal development but also strengthens one's relationship with Allah.

Lastly, seeking forgiveness from others plays a significant role in the process of repentance. Daily interactions provide numerous opportunities to mend relationships and address past grievances. Whether through a simple apology or a more profound reconciliation, these actions demonstrate humility and the desire to right wrongs. Engaging in acts of kindness and service to others also reflects a repentant heart, reaffirming one's commitment to living a life aligned with Islamic principles. By incorporating these daily practices of repentance, individuals can navigate life's trials with resilience and grace, ultimately enhancing their spiritual journey.

Incorporating At-Tawbah into Modern Life

Incorporating At-Tawbah into modern life requires an understanding of its principles and their application in various aspects of daily living. At-Tawbah, or repentance, emphasises the importance of seeking forgiveness from Allah for past mistakes and sins. This concept is not merely a ritual performed during specific times but rather a continuous process that can guide individuals through the complexities of contemporary challenges. By embracing the values of At-Tawbah, Muslims can foster a mindset that promotes personal growth, accountability, and resilience in the face of life's trials.

One of the key elements of At-Tawbah is the sincere intention to change and improve oneself. In today's fast-paced world, individuals often find themselves facing moral and ethical dilemmas. The act of repentance encourages Muslims to pause and reflect on their actions, guiding them toward making better choices. This reflective practice cultivates self-awareness and mindfulness, enabling individuals to recognise the impact of their decisions on themselves and others. By integrating this approach into modern life, Muslims can contribute positively to their communities and maintain a sense of integrity in their personal and professional relationships.

Furthermore, At-Tawbah reinforces the concept of community and the importance of social responsibility. In contemporary society, where individualism often takes precedence, the teachings of At-Tawbah remind Muslims of their duty towards others. Engaging in acts of kindness, seeking forgiveness from those they may have wronged, and being open to reconciliation are all manifestations of this principle. By actively participating in community service and supporting those in need, individuals embody the spirit of At-Tawbah, thus creating a more compassionate and cohesive society.

Technology and social media play a significant role in modern life, presenting both opportunities and challenges. The principles of At-Tawbah can be particularly relevant in this context, as they provide guidance on navigating the complexities of online interactions. Muslims can use these platforms to spread positivity, share knowledge, and offer support while being mindful of their words and actions. When mistakes occur, the call to repentance serves as a reminder to acknowledge errors and seek forgiveness, fostering a culture of accountability and humility in the digital sphere.

Lastly, the practice of At-Tawbah can serve as a source of comfort and hope during difficult times. Life's trials can lead to feelings of despair and isolation; however, the promise of Allah's mercy and forgiveness offers solace. By regularly engaging in the acts of repentance and seeking closeness to Allah, individuals can cultivate inner peace and resilience. This spiritual connection not only enhances personal well-being but also enables Muslims to face life's challenges with renewed strength and determination, embodying the essence of At-Tawbah in their everyday lives.

The Impact on Mental Health

The concept of At-Tawbah, or repentance, holds significant relevance in contemporary Muslim life, particularly in relation to mental health. As individuals navigate the complexities of modern existence, the principles surrounding repentance provide a framework for addressing feelings of guilt, anxiety, and emotional distress. Engaging in sincere repentance allows individuals to confront their missteps and seek forgiveness, fostering an environment conducive to healing and personal growth. This process can alleviate the burdens of past actions, leading to improved mental well-being.

Repentance encourages self-reflection, which is essential for mental health. By examining one's actions and intentions, individuals can gain insight into their behaviours and the impact these may have on their lives and the lives of others. This practice not only promotes accountability but also cultivates a sense of purpose and direction. When Muslims actively engage in At-Tawbah, they develop a deeper understanding of themselves, which can mitigate feelings of hopelessness and despair that often accompany mental health struggles.

Chapter 7:

At-Tawbah and Forgiveness

Moreover, the act of seeking forgiveness from Allah provides a powerful source of comfort and reassurance. Many individuals experience a sense of relief following the acknowledgement of their faults and the subsequent plea for pardon. This spiritual cleansing can lead to a reduction in anxiety and stress as believers recognise that they are not defined by their mistakes. The belief that Allah is merciful and forgiving can instill hope and positivity, transforming a negative mindset into one of resilience and strength.

Additionally, At-Tawbah promotes community and social support, which are critical components of mental health. Engaging in communal prayers and discussions about repentance fosters connections among individuals, creating a supportive network that can help alleviate feelings of isolation. This sense of belonging can be particularly beneficial for those struggling with mental health issues, as it reminds them that they are part of a larger community that shares similar beliefs and experiences.

In conclusion, the principles of At-Tawbah offer valuable insights into the relationship between faith and mental health. By embracing repentance, individuals can initiate a transformative journey that not only addresses their spiritual needs but also enhances their overall well-being. As Muslims face the trials of contemporary life, the practice of At-Tawbah serves as a reminder of the importance of self-reflection, forgiveness, and community, ultimately contributing to healthier minds and hearts.

Understanding Divine Forgiveness

Divine forgiveness is a concept that resonates deeply within the fabric of Islamic teachings, serving as a cornerstone of faith and personal development. Understanding divine forgiveness involves recognising its multifaceted nature, which encompasses mercy, compassion, and the opportunity for redemption. In Islam, Allah's forgiveness is boundless and often described as more generous than human comprehension. This notion encourages believers to seek repentance, reinforcing the idea that no sin is too great to be forgiven if approached with sincerity and a genuine resolve to amend one's ways.

At the heart of divine forgiveness lies the principle of Tawbah, or repentance. Tawbah is not merely a verbal expression of remorse but an active commitment to change behaviour and seek a closer relationship with Allah. This process requires self-reflection, acknowledgement of one's wrongdoings, and a firm intention to avoid repeating those mistakes. The act of repenting is vital for spiritual growth, as it allows individuals to confront their faults and transform their lives in accordance with divine will.

Understanding this process is essential for Muslims navigating the complexities of contemporary life, where distractions and temptations can easily lead one astray.

In contemporary society, the relevance of divine forgiveness is particularly pronounced. Many individuals grapple with feelings of guilt, shame, and inadequacy due to their actions or circumstances. The notion that divine forgiveness is accessible can provide significant relief and hope. It fosters resilience, encouraging individuals to rise above their past and pursue a life aligned with their values. This understanding helps cultivate a forgiving spirit, not only towards oneself but also towards others, promoting a culture of empathy and compassion in communities.

Furthermore, divine forgiveness emphasises the importance of accountability. It teaches that seeking forgiveness is not a means to escape consequences but rather a way to own one's actions and strive for improvement. This aspect is especially relevant in today's world, where accountability is often overlooked. By embracing the principles of Tawbah and divine forgiveness, individuals can learn to navigate their mistakes with integrity, ensuring that personal growth is rooted in honesty and self-awareness.

Ultimately, understanding divine forgiveness fosters a sense of hope and renewal. It reassures believers that, regardless of their past, they can always return to Allah with a sincere heart. This dynamic interplay between sin, repentance, and forgiveness is not only foundational to Islamic doctrine but also serves as a guiding light for Muslims facing life's trials. By internalising these principles, individuals can navigate their spiritual journeys with confidence, resilience, and a profound sense of purpose, reinforcing the relevance of At-Tawbah in their lives.

Forgiving Others

Forgiveness is a fundamental concept in many cultures and religions, and in Islam, it holds a special significance. The act of forgiving others is not merely a moral choice but a spiritual obligation that aligns with the teachings of At-Tawbah, or repentance. Forgiving others can be a transformative experience, allowing individuals to release the burden of resentment and anger that can weigh heavily on the heart. It fosters personal growth, enhances interpersonal relationships, and creates a sense of community and harmony within society.

In Islam, forgiveness is deeply rooted in the belief that human beings are fallible. The Quran emphasises the importance of mercy and compassion, encouraging believers to forgive those who have wronged them. This divine perspective reminds Muslims that just as they seek forgiveness from Allah for their own sins, they must also extend that same mercy to others. The act of forgiving is not about condoning wrongdoing; rather, it is about liberating oneself from the shackles of negativity and choosing a path of peace and understanding.

The process of forgiving others can sometimes be challenging, especially when the hurt is profound. However, it is essential to recognise that holding onto grudges can lead to spiritual and emotional turmoil. In contrast, forgiveness can lead to healing and reconciliation. By practising forgiveness, individuals can cultivate a sense of empathy, understanding the circumstances that may have led to the actions of others. This shift in perspective can ease the pain and pave the way for a more harmonious existence.

Moreover, forgiving others is not only beneficial for the one who is forgiven but also for the one who extends forgiveness. It can enhance psychological well-being, reduce stress, and promote a sense of inner peace. In the context of At-Tawbah, practising forgiveness aligns with the principles of humility and self-reflection. It encourages individuals to examine their own faults and shortcomings while fostering a spirit of community and support among fellow Muslims. Thus, forgiveness becomes a means of nurturing a compassionate society.

In conclusion, the act of forgiving others is a vital aspect of personal and communal well- being in Islamic teachings. It embodies the essence of At-Tawbah, reinforcing the idea that while humans may err, they also have the capacity for mercy and forgiveness. By embracing forgiveness, Muslims can navigate life's trials with resilience and grace, ultimately fostering a more harmonious and understanding world. In doing so, they not only adhere to their faith but also contribute positively to the broader society, creating an environment where healing and compassion thrive.

The Power of Forgiveness in Relationships

Forgiveness stands as a cornerstone in the foundation of healthy relationships, serving as a crucial element in the journey of personal growth and communal harmony. In the context of At-Tawbah, or repentance, forgiveness embodies not just an individual act but a collective healing process that can transform the dynamics between individuals. This is particularly significant for Muslims navigating the complexities of contemporary life, where misunderstandings and conflicts can arise in both personal and communal spheres. Embracing forgiveness allows individuals to move beyond grievances, fostering a spirit of reconciliation that is essential for maintaining strong, supportive relationships.

The act of forgiving requires a conscious decision to release resentment and anger towards those who have wronged us. In Islamic teachings, forgiveness is not merely an option; it is a virtue that is highly encouraged and often rewarded. The Quran emphasises the importance of forgiving others, highlighting that those who forgive will be granted mercy. This divine perspective serves as a guiding principle for Muslims, urging them to adopt a forgiving attitude, which can lead to personal liberation from negative emotions. By practising forgiveness, individuals can cultivate an environment of trust and understanding, essential for nurturing relationships.

Moreover, forgiveness can significantly improve emotional and mental well-being. Holding onto grudges can lead to bitterness and stress, affecting one's health and overall quality of life. In contrast, the act of forgiving can release burdens that weigh heavily on the heart and mind. This process aligns with the Islamic understanding of At-Tawbah, where seeking forgiveness from Allah also involves forgiving others. By letting go of past grievances, individuals find peace and clarity, allowing them to focus on building stronger connections with those around them. This personal healing contributes to a more compassionate and empathetic community.

In relationships, the power of forgiveness can mend rifts and foster deeper connections. When one partner extends forgiveness to another, it not only repairs the immediate conflict but also strengthens the bond between them. This mutual understanding can lead to improved communication and collaboration, essential elements for relationship longevity. For Muslims, practising forgiveness is a reflection of their faith and commitment to embodying the principles of compassion and mercy taught by the Prophet Muhammad. Such actions not only enhance personal relationships but also serve as a model for others, promoting a culture of forgiveness within the wider community.

Ultimately, the power of forgiveness in relationships is intertwined with the principles of At-Tawbah. It represents a continuous cycle of repentance, healing, and renewal. By actively engaging in forgiveness, individuals not only fulfil their spiritual obligations but also contribute to a more harmonious society. In a world rife with conflict and division, the practice of forgiveness emerges as a vital tool, enabling individuals to navigate their trials with grace and resilience. This commitment to forgiveness encourages a collective movement towards understanding and unity, reflecting the essence of Muslim identity in contemporary life.

Chapter 8:

The Future of At-Tawbah in Muslim Life

Challenges Facing Contemporary Muslims

Contemporary Muslims face a myriad of challenges that impact their daily lives and spiritual practices. One significant challenge is the perception of Islam in a global context, particularly in the wake of geopolitical events that have often painted Muslims in a negative light. Media portrayals, often focusing on extremism and terrorism, can lead to widespread misunderstanding and prejudice. This misrepresentation not only affects the way Muslims are viewed by others but also influences how they view themselves, potentially leading to internalised stigma and a sense of isolation within their communities.

Another challenge is the struggle for identity in increasingly multicultural societies. Many Muslims find themselves navigating their religious obligations while simultaneously adapting to the cultural norms of their non-Muslim environments. This balancing act can create tension, especially for younger generations who may feel pressure to conform to societal expectations while trying to maintain their religious identity. The quest for acceptance can lead to conflicts in values, making it difficult for individuals to reconcile their faith with the secular influences that surround them.

Economic disparities also play a critical role in the challenges faced by contemporary Muslims. Many communities experience higher rates of poverty and unemployment, which can hinder access to education and opportunities for advancement. This economic struggle can lead to feelings of disenfranchisement and frustration, particularly when combined with a lack of representation in various sectors. The challenges associated with economic hardship often result in a sense of hopelessness, which can further complicate the pursuit of spiritual and personal growth.

Additionally, the rise of digital technology presents both opportunities and challenges for Muslims today. While the internet offers a platform for education and community building, it can also expose individuals to misinformation and extremist ideologies.

Navigating the vast amount of information available online can be daunting, especially for young Muslims seeking guidance on their faith. The challenge lies in discerning authentic sources of Islamic knowledge from those that promote division or radicalisation, making it essential for communities to foster critical thinking and media literacy.

Finally, the issue of mental health is increasingly relevant within Muslim communities, yet it often remains stigmatised. Many individuals face mental health challenges, exacerbated by societal pressures, discrimination, and the struggle to maintain a balance between faith and modern life. However, discussions around mental health can be fraught with cultural taboos, making it difficult for individuals to seek help. Addressing mental health openly within the framework of Islamic teachings can encourage a more supportive environment that promotes well-being while reinforcing the importance of seeking help as a part of one's faith journey.

The Relevance of At-Tawbah in a Changing World

The concept of At-Tawbah, or repentance, holds a profound significance in the lives of Muslims, especially in a rapidly changing world. Its relevance transcends mere religious obligation; it embodies a pathway to personal growth and societal healing. In an era where moral and ethical dilemmas are increasingly prevalent, the principles of At-Tawbah provide a framework for individuals seeking to navigate their challenges while fostering a sense of accountability. This chapter explores how At-Tawbah serves as a guiding light in contemporary life, encouraging self-reflection and a commitment to positive transformation.

In today's society, where individuals are often confronted with conflicting values and pressures, the act of repentance offers a moment of pause. It prompts believers to assess their actions, seek forgiveness, and strive for improvement. This process not only nurtures personal integrity but also strengthens community bonds. As Muslims engage with the tenets of At-Tawbah, they cultivate an environment of mutual support and understanding, reinforcing the idea that everyone is on a continuous journey of self-discovery and rectification.

The teachings surrounding At-Tawbah emphasise that the door to repentance is always open, regardless of the gravity of one's misdeeds. This principle is particularly relevant today, as many individuals grapple with feelings of guilt, shame, and despair stemming from their actions. By understanding that repentance is not just an act of seeking forgiveness, but also a means of reclaiming one's dignity, individuals can nd solace in their struggles. The message that no one is beyond redemption can inspire hope and motivate individuals to rise above their circumstances, leading to personal and spiritual renewal.

Moreover, the application of At-Tawbah extends beyond the individual to encompass broader societal implications. In a world rife with injustice, inequality, and conflict, the principles of repentance encourage collective accountability. Communities that embrace the spirit of At-Tawbah can work together to rectify wrongs, promote justice, and foster reconciliation. This communal approach reinforces the notion that societal change begins with individual commitment, urging Muslims to address not only their personal shortcomings but also the challenges facing their communities.

Finally, the relevance of At-Tawbah in a changing world lies in its potential to bridge the gap between tradition and modernity. As Muslims navigate contemporary issues—such as mental health, social justice, and environmental stewardship—the principles of repentance can provide a moral compass. By integrating At-Tawbah into their lives, individuals can approach modern challenges with a renewed perspective, grounded in the values of humility, compassion, and resilience. Thus, At-Tawbah remains a timeless and essential aspect of the Muslim experience, guiding believers in their quest for personal fulfilment and collective advancement in an ever-evolving landscape.

Inspiring Future Generations

Inspiring future generations is a crucial aspect of ensuring that the values and lessons derived from At-Tawbah resonate beyond our own lifetimes. The chapter emphasises the importance of instilling a sense of purpose, responsibility, and resilience in young Muslims. By understanding the themes of forgiveness, accountability, and the importance of community found within At-Tawbah, future generations can navigate their own trials with a sense of direction and strength. This guidance not only shapes their personal character but also impacts their interactions with the wider world, promoting a more compassionate and understanding society.

At-Tawbah serves as a reminder that challenges are an intrinsic part of life. By sharing stories of perseverance and the significance of seeking forgiveness, adults can provide a framework for young Muslims to handle their own difficulties. The chapter encourages mentors, parents, and educators to highlight the relevance of these teachings in daily experiences. By relating the lessons from At-Tawbah to real-life situations, young individuals can grasp the importance of resilience and the power of repentance, fostering a growth mindset that embraces learning from mistakes.

Moreover, the chapter discusses the importance of role models in inspiring future generations. Figures from Islamic history, who exemplified the virtues of At-Tawbah, provide relatable examples for young Muslims. By exploring the lives of these individuals, young people gain insight into how to embody the principles of repentance and social responsibility in their own lives. This connection to historical figures not only enriches their understanding of their faith but also empowers them to take on challenges with the same determination and faith.

Community involvement is another vital aspect addressed in the chapter. Encouraging young Muslims to engage with their communities fosters a sense of belonging and responsibility. At-Tawbah emphasises the need for collective support and accountability, and by participating in community service or social justice initiatives, young individuals can put these teachings into practice. The chapter highlights how such experiences can shape their identities, instilling a commitment to contribute positively to society while reinforcing the importance of solidarity and compassion.

Lastly, the chapter underscores the role of education in inspiring future generations. By integrating the teachings of At-Tawbah into educational curricula, educators can create an environment where students learn not only about their faith but also about the broader moral and ethical implications of their actions. This holistic approach to education equips young Muslims with the tools necessary to navigate contemporary challenges while remaining grounded in their spiritual identity. By fostering a culture of learning that emphasises the relevance of At-Tawbah, we can inspire future generations to lead lives marked by integrity, empathy, and resilience.

Chapter 9:

Conclusion: Embracing At-Tawbah

The Ongoing Journey of Repentance

Repentance, or At-Tawbah, is not merely a momentary act of seeking forgiveness; it is an ongoing journey that shapes a Muslim's life. This journey begins with a recognition of one's shortcomings and a sincere desire to return to the right path. The Quran emphasises the importance of repentance, encouraging believers to turn back to Allah with humility and sincerity. This process involves acknowledging one's sins, feeling genuine remorse, and making a steadfast intention not to return to those actions. It is a holistic approach that encompasses the mind, heart, and actions, reinforcing the idea that repentance is a continual state rather than a one-time event.

As individuals navigate the complexities of contemporary life, the relevance of At-Tawbah becomes increasingly evident. In a world filled with distractions and moral challenges, the ability to seek forgiveness and recalibrate one's life is essential. The ongoing journey of repentance allows Muslims to confront their mistakes and engage with their faith actively. It acts as a spiritual reset, providing the opportunity to reflect on one's actions and their impact on oneself and others. This journey fosters resilience, encouraging believers to rise above their failures and strive for personal and spiritual growth.

Moreover, the communal aspect of repentance cannot be overlooked. In Islamic tradition, seeking forgiveness is often accompanied by making amends with others. Engaging in acts of kindness and restoring relationships enhances the process of At-Tawbah. This collective dimension reinforces community bonds, as individuals support one another in their journeys of repentance. The shared experience of seeking forgiveness creates an environment where accountability and compassion thrive, reminding everyone of the importance of empathy in personal and communal healing.

The ongoing journey of repentance also encourages self-awareness and mindfulness. As Muslims reflect on their actions, they become more attuned to their behaviour and its consequences. This heightened self-awareness leads to better decision-making and a more intentional approach to life. By consistently evaluating their choices, believers can cultivate habits that align with their values and beliefs. The journey of At-Tawbah, therefore, becomes a catalyst for positive change, guiding individuals toward a life that embodies the principles of Islam.

Ultimately, the journey of repentance is a path toward inner peace and spiritual fulfilment. It invites individuals to embrace their imperfections while striving for improvement. Through At-Tawbah, Muslims are reminded that they are never beyond the reach of Allah's mercy. This ongoing commitment to seeking forgiveness nurtures a deeper connection with the Divine, fostering a sense of hope and purpose in the face of life's trials. As believers continue on this journey, they not only transform their own lives but also contribute to a more compassionate and understanding world.

Living with Intention and Purpose

Living with intention and purpose is a fundamental aspect of navigating life's trials, particularly within the framework of Islamic teachings. The concept of intention, or niyyah, is deeply rooted in the practices of a Muslim's daily life. It serves as a guiding principle that shapes actions, decisions, and interactions with others. By cultivating a mindset centred on intention, individuals can transform mundane activities into acts of worship, thereby infusing their lives with deeper meaning and relevance. This perspective is especially significant in the context of At-Tawbah, which emphasises the importance of sincere repentance and the rectification of one's path.

At-Tawbah highlights the notion that every individual has the capacity to realign their life towards a purpose that resonates with their values and beliefs. The act of turning back to God, or Tawbah, encourages self-reflection and accountability. In contemporary Muslim life, where distractions and challenges abound, living with intention becomes a powerful tool for personal growth. It prompts individuals to evaluate their choices and habits, ensuring that they are in harmony with Islamic principles. This conscious approach to living not only enhances spiritual fulfilment but also fosters resilience in the face of life's adversities.

Incorporating intention into daily routines can take many forms, from setting clear goals to engaging in community service. Practising gratitude and mindfulness in everyday actions allows individuals to remain focused on their purpose. For instance, when performing prayers or engaging in charitable acts, a mindful approach can deepen the spiritual significance of these rituals. By consciously aligning actions with the core tenets of Islam, such as compassion and humility, Muslims can cultivate a life that reflects their commitment to faith. This alignment not only enriches their personal experiences but also positively impacts their communities and those around them.

Additionally, living with purpose encourages individuals to seek knowledge and personal development. The pursuit of knowledge is a highly valued principle in Islam; it empowers individuals to make informed decisions and fosters a sense of responsibility towards oneself and society. By prioritising education and self-improvement, Muslims can better equip themselves to navigate the complexities of modern life. This journey of continuous learning is intricately tied to the themes of At-Tawbah, as it reinforces the idea that one can always strive for betterment and seek forgiveness for past shortcomings.

Ultimately, living with intention and purpose is about embracing the journey of life with a proactive mindset. It encourages individuals to take ownership of their paths, recognising that every choice has the potential to bring them closer to their spiritual goals. By reflecting on the lessons of At-Tawbah, Muslims can draw inspiration to live authentically and with conviction. In a world filled with uncertainty, the clarity that comes from living intentionally allows for a more meaningful existence, where each moment is an opportunity for growth, connection, and fulfilment in God's service.

Final Reflections on At-Tawbah

At-Tawbah, or "The Repentance," stands as a vital chapter in the Quran, emphasising the themes of forgiveness, accountability, and the importance of returning to one's faith. In contemporary life, where distractions and trials abound, the messages contained within this chapter encourage Muslims to reflect on their actions and intentions. It serves as a reminder that despite the challenges faced, there is always a pathway back to righteousness through sincere repentance. This chapter calls upon believers to actively engage with their faith, ensuring that their actions align with Islamic principles.

One of the central tenets of At-Tawbah is the notion of accountability. In a world increasingly characterised by moral ambiguity and ethical dilemmas, the chapter urges individuals to evaluate their choices and the impact of those choices on their spiritual well-being. It emphasises that each person is responsible for their actions, and this accountability extends beyond mere compliance with religious obligations. Instead, it invites deeper introspection about one's relationship with God and the sincerity of one's intentions. This reflection is particularly relevant in today's society, where external influences can often lead individuals away from their core values.

Moreover, At-Tawbah addresses the importance of community and collective responsibility. The chapter underscores that the journey of repentance is not solely an individual endeavour; rather, it involves a communal aspect where believers support one another in their quests for spiritual growth. In contemporary Muslim life, fostering a sense of community can combat feelings of isolation and despair that often accompany life's trials. The teachings within At-Tawbah encourage Muslims to engage in communal prayers, charity, and mutual support, reinforcing the idea that collective efforts can lead to societal improvement and personal healing.

The concept of hope is also a pivotal theme in At-Tawbah, reminding individuals that no matter how far one may stray from the path of righteousness, there is always an opportunity for redemption. This message is particularly powerful in a time when many may feel overwhelmed by their shortcomings or the trials they face. It encourages believers to maintain faith in God's mercy and to actively seek forgiveness, reinforcing the idea that personal growth is a continuous journey. By embracing this hope, individuals can navigate their challenges with resilience and a renewed sense of purpose.

In conclusion, At-Tawbah serves as a profound source of guidance for Muslims navigating the complexities of modern life. Its teachings on accountability, community, and hope are essential in fostering a deeper understanding of one's faith amid contemporary challenges. As individuals reflect on the chapter's messages, they are reminded of the importance of sincere repentance and the transformative power it holds. Embracing these lessons can lead to a more fulfilling spiritual journey, reinforcing the relevance of At-Tawbah in today's world.

www.ingramcontent.com/pod-product-compliance
Lightning Source LLC
Chambersburg PA
CBHW061129070526
44584CB00033B/4272